God Wants Me to Be Rich

DIANA GADUS, M.ED.

God Wants Me to Be Rich

Diana Gadus, M.Ed.

God Wants Me to Be Rich

God Wants Me to Be Rich

Authored by: Diana Gadus, M.Ed.

God Wants Me to Be Rich

Diana Gadus, Inc

8711 Wesleyan Dr

Fort Myers, Fl 33919

THE HOLY BIBLE, NEW INTERNATIONAL VERSION®, NIV® Copyright © 1973, 1978, 1984, 2011 by Biblica, Inc.® Used by permission. All rights reserved worldwide.

Diana Gadus, M.Ed.

Preface

In a world where the pursuit of wealth often appears to be in direct conflict with spiritual values, many believers find themselves grappling with a profound question: *Is it truly God's will for me to be wealthy?* This book, "God Wants Me to Be Rich," is born out of the desire to address this question by turning to the source of all truth—the Word of God.

From the very beginning, God's relationship with humanity has been marked by His desire to bless us abundantly. The Bible is replete with stories of individuals who walked in God's favor and experienced tremendous blessings, not just in their spiritual lives but also in their material wealth. Yet, the notion of wealth has often been misunderstood, even within the Christian community. Some equate wealth with greed or materialism, while others struggle with a poverty mindset, believing that true piety requires living with less.

This book seeks to dismantle these misconceptions and present a biblical understanding of wealth that is both balanced and life-affirming. It is not a call to greed or excess, but a call to embrace the fullness of God's blessings with gratitude, responsibility, and purpose. It is about understanding that wealth, when pursued and managed according to biblical principles, is a tool for advancing God's kingdom, blessing others, and fulfilling our God-given potential.

Diana Gadus, M.Ed.

God Wants Me to Be Rich

In the pages that follow, we will journey through the Scriptures to uncover the divine principles that guide wealth creation and management. We will explore the importance of faith, stewardship, generosity, and ethical wealth building, and we will address the spiritual warfare that often accompanies the pursuit of prosperity. Through practical steps and real-life testimonies, this book aims to equip you with the knowledge and tools needed to align your financial life with God's will.

As you read, I encourage you to approach this book with an open heart and mind, ready to embrace the truths that God has for you. Whether you are just beginning your financial journey or are already well on your way, I believe that the principles in this book will help you deepen your understanding of God's will for your prosperity and inspire you to live a life of abundance that honors Him.

May this book be a source of encouragement, wisdom, and inspiration as you seek to experience the fullness of God's blessings in every area of your life. Remember, wealth is not an end in itself, but a means to glorify God and to make a lasting impact in the world. As you apply these principles, I pray that you will walk in the abundant life that Jesus promised—a life marked by purpose, fulfillment, and the joy of knowing that you are living according to God's perfect plan.

With faith and hope,

Diana Gadus, M.Ed.

Diana Gadus, M.Ed.

Table Of Contents

Diana Gadus, M.Ed.

Chapter 1: Wealth in the Kingdom of God

Diana Gadus, M.Ed.

In the quest for understanding wealth from a biblical perspective, we begin by exploring the concept of wealth within the Kingdom of God. It is crucial to establish that God's view on wealth significantly differs from the world's view. In the secular realm, wealth is often pursued for personal gain, status, and power. However, in God's Kingdom, wealth is seen as a tool to fulfill His divine purposes and to bless others.

The Bible provides numerous examples of godly individuals who were blessed with substantial wealth. These stories are not merely historical accounts but are lessons and encouragement for believers today. Let us delve deeper into these examples and the principles they embody.

Abraham: The Patriarch of Faith and Wealth

Abraham, known as the father of faith, is one of the most prominent figures in the Bible. He was also a man of great wealth. Genesis 13:2 states, "Abram had become very wealthy in livestock and in silver and gold." Abraham's wealth was not just a result of his hard work but a direct blessing from God. God promised to bless Abraham and make him a great nation (Genesis 12:2-3), and this promise included material wealth.

Abraham's story teaches us several important lessons about wealth:

Diana Gadus, M.Ed.

God Wants Me to Be Rich

1. Obedience to God: Abraham's wealth was a result of his obedience to God's call. When God asked him to leave his homeland and go to a land that He would show him, Abraham obeyed without hesitation (Genesis 12:1-4). This act of obedience positioned him to receive God's blessings.
2. Faith in God's Promises: Abraham believed in God's promises even when they seemed impossible. His faith was counted to him as righteousness (Genesis 15:6). Faith in God's promises is essential for receiving His blessings, including financial prosperity.
3. Generosity: Abraham was generous and hospitable. In Genesis 18, we see him welcoming three visitors and providing them with food and rest. This act of kindness led to the reaffirmation of God's promise to him. Generosity is a key principle in the Kingdom of God that unlocks further blessings.

Solomon: Wisdom and Wealth

King Solomon, the son of David, is another notable example of godly wealth. When Solomon became king, God appeared to him in a dream and asked him what he wanted. Solomon asked for wisdom to govern God's people (1 Kings 3:5-9). Pleased with his request, God granted him unparalleled wisdom and also blessed him with riches and honor (1 Kings 3:10-13).

Solomon's story highlights several principles:

Diana Gadus, M.Ed.

1. Seeking God's Wisdom: Solomon's wealth was a byproduct of his desire for wisdom. Proverbs 3:13-14 states, "Blessed are those who find wisdom, those who gain understanding, for she is more profitable than silver and yields better returns than gold." Seeking God's wisdom is crucial for financial prosperity.
2. Using Wealth for God's Glory: Solomon used his wealth to build the temple of the Lord, a place of worship and sacrifice (1 Kings 6). Our wealth should be used to advance God's kingdom and bring glory to His name.
3. The Dangers of Wealth: Solomon's later years serve as a cautionary tale. Despite his wisdom, he allowed wealth and foreign influences to lead him away from God (1 Kings 11:1-6). This reminds us to remain vigilant and guard our hearts against the potential pitfalls of wealth.

Job: Faithfulness and Restoration

Job's story is unique in that it encompasses both immense wealth and extreme loss. Job was a man of great wealth and integrity. However, he lost everything in a series of devastating events (Job 1-2). Despite his suffering, Job remained faithful to God. In the end, God restored Job's fortunes, giving him twice as much as he had before (Job 42:10).

From Job's life, we learn:

Diana Gadus, M.Ed.

1. Faithfulness in Adversity: Job's faithfulness during his trials is exemplary. His story teaches us to trust God even when we face financial difficulties, knowing that He is in control and has a plan for our restoration.
2. God's Sovereignty: Job's restoration was a testament to God's sovereignty and faithfulness. It reassures us that God can turn our situations around and bless us beyond our expectations.

The Purpose of Wealth in the Kingdom of God

The examples of Abraham, Solomon, and Job illustrate that wealth in the Kingdom of God is not merely about accumulation but about fulfilling God's purposes. Here are some key purposes of wealth in God's Kingdom:

1. Advancing God's Kingdom: Wealth should be used to support ministries, missions, and the spread of the gospel. In Matthew 28:19-20, Jesus commissioned His disciples to make disciples of all nations. Financial resources are essential for fulfilling this Great Commission.

2. Blessing Others: God blesses us so that we can be a blessing to others. Proverbs 11:25 says, "A generous person will prosper; whoever refreshes others will be refreshed." Generosity reflects God's heart and opens the door for more blessings.

Diana Gadus, M.Ed.

3. Providing for Our Families: 1 Timothy 5:8 emphasizes the importance of providing for our families. Wealth enables us to meet the needs of our loved ones and ensure their well-being.

4. Living a Life of Integrity: Wealth gained through honest means and managed with integrity honors God. Proverbs 13:11 states, "Dishonest money dwindles away, but whoever gathers money little by little makes it grow."

5. Demonstrating God's Goodness: Our prosperity can serve as a testimony to God's goodness and faithfulness. When others see God's blessings in our lives, it can draw them closer to Him.

Conclusion

Wealth in the Kingdom of God is a multifaceted concept that encompasses obedience, faith, generosity, wisdom, and integrity. By understanding and applying these principles, we position ourselves to receive God's blessings and use them for His glory. As we journey through the subsequent chapters, we will delve deeper into these principles and learn how to align our financial practices with God's will. Remember, God's desire is not just for us to be wealthy but to be prosperous in a way that honors Him and advances His kingdom.

Diana Gadus, M.Ed.

Chapter 2: The Biblical Foundation of Wealth

Diana Gadus, M.Ed.

To truly understand and embrace the concept of wealth in the Kingdom of God, we must first lay a solid foundation based on biblical teachings. The Bible provides comprehensive guidance on how to acquire, manage, and utilize wealth in a manner that aligns with God's will. This chapter will explore the biblical foundation of wealth, examining key scriptures and principles that form the bedrock of our understanding.

The Creation Mandate and Dominion

Our journey begins in the Book of Genesis, where God created the heavens and the earth. In Genesis 1:26-28, God said, "Let us make mankind in our image, in our likeness, so that they may rule over the fish in the sea and the birds in the sky, over the livestock and all the wild animals, and over all the creatures that move along the ground." God blessed humanity and gave them dominion over the earth, entrusting them with the responsibility to steward His creation.

This mandate to exercise dominion is foundational to our understanding of wealth. God endowed humanity with the authority to manage and cultivate the earth's resources. This includes the creation of wealth through agriculture, trade, and industry. The ability to produce wealth is a divine gift, and our stewardship of these resources reflects our obedience to God's original design.

Diana Gadus, M.Ed.

The Covenant with Abraham

The covenant God made with Abraham is another critical element in the biblical foundation of wealth. In Genesis 12:2-3, God promised Abraham, "I will make you into a great nation, and I will bless you; I will make your name great, and you will be a blessing. I will bless those who bless you, and whoever curses you I will curse; and all peoples on earth will be blessed through you."

This covenant underscores that God's blessing extends beyond spiritual well-being to include material prosperity. Abraham's wealth was a tangible expression of God's favor and a means through which he could bless others. This principle is reaffirmed in Galatians 3:14, which states that the blessings of Abraham come to the Gentiles through Christ Jesus. As heirs to this covenant, we are recipients of God's promise of prosperity.

The Role of Obedience and Faith

Throughout the Bible, obedience to God's commandments and faith in His promises are repeatedly linked to material blessings. Deuteronomy 28:1-14 outlines the blessings that come from obeying God's commands, including prosperity in the city and the country, abundant crops, and successful enterprises. Verse 8 specifically promises, "The Lord will send a blessing on your barns and on everything you put your hand to."

Diana Gadus, M.Ed.

Faith, as exemplified by Abraham, is another key component. Hebrews 11:1 defines faith as "confidence in what we hope for and assurance about what we do not see." This chapter will explore how faith and obedience are critical to unlocking God's promises of wealth and prosperity.

The Principle of Stewardship

Stewardship is a central theme in the Bible and is essential for understanding how to manage wealth in a way that honors God. The Parable of the Talents (Matthew 25:14-30) illustrates the importance of being faithful stewards of the resources God entrusts to us. In this parable, the master entrusts his servants with varying amounts of money before going on a journey. Upon his return, he rewards the servants who wisely invested and multiplied their resources and punishes the one who did nothing with his share.

This parable teaches us that God expects us to be proactive and diligent in managing our resources. Stewardship involves recognizing that everything we have belongs to God and that we are accountable for how we use it. Proper stewardship leads to increased blessings and greater responsibilities.

Generosity and Tithing

Generosity is a key principle that reflects God's heart. Proverbs 11:25 states, "A generous person will prosper; whoever refreshes others will be refreshed." The Bible consistently encourages believers to be generous and to share their blessings with others. Acts 20:35 reminds us of Jesus' words, "It is more blessed to give than to receive."

Tithing, or giving a tenth of one's income, is another biblical principle related to wealth. In Malachi 3:10, God challenges His people to "bring the whole tithe into the storehouse" and promises to "open the floodgates of heaven and pour out so much blessing that there will not be room enough to store it." Tithing is an act of faith and obedience that acknowledges God's provision and sovereignty.

Wisdom and Prudence

The Bible places a high value on wisdom and prudence, especially in financial matters. Proverbs 3:13-14 states, "Blessed are those who find wisdom, those who gain understanding, for she is more profitable than silver and yields better returns than gold." Wisdom guides us in making sound financial decisions, avoiding debt, and investing wisely.

Diana Gadus, M.Ed.

The Book of Proverbs is filled with practical advice on managing wealth. Proverbs 21:5 teaches, "The plans of the diligent lead to profit as surely as haste leads to poverty." This highlights the importance of careful planning and diligent work in achieving financial success.

The Danger of Loving Money

While the Bible supports the pursuit of wealth, it also warns against the love of money. 1 Timothy 6:10 cautions, "For the love of money is a root of all kinds of evil. Some people, eager for money, have wandered from the faith and pierced themselves with many griefs." This warning serves as a reminder that our focus should be on God and His purposes, rather than on accumulating wealth for its own sake.

Wealth as a Testimony of God's Goodness

Finally, wealth can serve as a testimony of God's goodness and faithfulness. When others see God's blessings in our lives, it can draw them closer to Him. Deuteronomy 8:18 reminds us, "But remember the Lord your God, for it is he who gives you the ability to produce wealth, and so confirms his covenant, which he swore to your ancestors, as it is today."

Diana Gadus, M.Ed.

By living out these principles, we demonstrate that God's ways lead to prosperity and that His promises are true. Our wealth becomes a powerful testimony of His provision and a tool for advancing His kingdom.

Conclusion

The biblical foundation of wealth is built on principles of dominion, covenant blessings, obedience, faith, stewardship, generosity, wisdom, and the right attitude towards money. By understanding and applying these principles, we align ourselves with God's will and position ourselves to receive His blessings. As we continue our journey through this book, we will explore each of these principles in greater depth, providing practical insights and applications to help you experience the fullness of God's prosperity in your life.

Diana Gadus, M.Ed.

God Wants Me to Be Rich

Diana Gadus, M.Ed.

Chapter 3: Understanding God's Will for Prosperity

Diana Gadus, M.Ed.

God Wants Me to Be Rich

In our exploration of wealth from a biblical perspective, it is essential to understand God's will for prosperity. Prosperity in the Kingdom of God encompasses more than just financial abundance; it includes spiritual, emotional, and physical well-being. This chapter will delve into the scriptural basis for God's desire for our prosperity and how we can align ourselves with His will to experience His blessings.

The Comprehensive Nature of Prosperity

God's vision of prosperity is holistic. It is not limited to material wealth but includes every aspect of our lives. 3 John 1:2 expresses this beautifully: "Beloved, I pray that you may prosper in all things and be in health, just as your soul prospers." This verse highlights that true prosperity is multifaceted, encompassing our physical health, financial stability, and spiritual well-being.

God's Promises of Prosperity

The Bible is filled with promises of prosperity for those who follow God's ways. These promises are not just empty words but are backed by God's faithfulness and power. Let us examine some key scriptures that reveal God's will for our prosperity:

Diana Gadus, M.Ed.

God Wants Me to Be Rich

1. Jeremiah 29:11: "For I know the plans I have for you," declares the Lord, "plans to prosper you and not to harm you, plans to give you hope and a future." This verse reassures us that God's plans for us are rooted in His desire for our prosperity and well-being.

2. Psalm 35:27: "Let them shout for joy and be glad, who favor my righteous cause; and let them say continually, 'Let the Lord be magnified, who has pleasure in the prosperity of His servant.'" God takes pleasure in our prosperity because it reflects His goodness and faithfulness.

3. Deuteronomy 8:18: "But remember the Lord your God, for it is he who gives you the ability to produce wealth, and so confirms his covenant, which he swore to your ancestors, as it is today." This verse underscores that the ability to create wealth is a divine gift and a confirmation of God's covenant with us.

4. Isaiah 48:17: "This is what the Lord says—your Redeemer, the Holy One of Israel: 'I am the Lord your God, who teaches you what is best for you, who directs you in the way you should go.'" God's guidance and teachings are aimed at leading us towards prosperity.

Diana Gadus, M.Ed.

The Purpose of Prosperity

Understanding the purpose of prosperity is crucial for aligning ourselves with God's will. Prosperity is not an end in itself but a means to fulfill God's purposes on Earth. Here are some key purposes of prosperity:

1. Advancing God's Kingdom: Financial resources are essential for supporting ministries, missions, and the spread of the gospel. In Matthew 28:19-20, Jesus commissioned His disciples to make disciples of all nations. Prosperity enables us to contribute to this Great Commission.

2. Blessing Others: God blesses us so that we can be a blessing to others. Proverbs 11:25 states, "A generous person will prosper; whoever refreshes others will be refreshed." Generosity reflects God's heart and opens the door for more blessings.

3. Living a Life of Abundance: John 10:10b says, "I have come that they may have life, and have it to the full." Jesus came to give us an abundant life, and prosperity is a part of this fullness.

4. Demonstrating God's Goodness: Our prosperity serves as a testimony of God's goodness and faithfulness. When others see His blessings in our lives, it can draw them closer to Him.

Diana Gadus, M.Ed.

Aligning with God's Will for Prosperity

To experience God's prosperity, we must align ourselves with His will. This involves several key steps:

1. Seeking God's Kingdom First: Matthew 6:33 instructs us to "seek first his kingdom and his righteousness, and all these things will be given to you as well." Prioritizing God's kingdom and righteousness is essential for experiencing His blessings.

2. Walking in Obedience: Deuteronomy 28:1-14 outlines the blessings that come from obeying God's commands. Obedience is a key factor in unlocking God's promises of prosperity.

3. Exercising Faith: Hebrews 11:6 reminds us that "without faith it is impossible to please God." Faith is critical for receiving God's blessings, including financial prosperity.

4. Practicing Stewardship: Proper stewardship involves managing our resources wisely and responsibly. The Parable of the Talents (Matthew 25:14-30) teaches us the importance of being faithful stewards.

5. Cultivating Generosity: Generosity is a powerful principle that aligns us with God's heart. Luke 6:38 says, "Give, and it will be given to you. A good measure, pressed down, shaken together and running over, will be poured into your lap."

Diana Gadus, M.Ed.

6. Trusting in God's Timing: Ecclesiastes 3:1 reminds us that "there is a time for everything, and a season for every activity under the heavens." Trusting in God's timing is essential for experiencing His prosperity.

Overcoming Hindrances to Prosperity

There are several hindrances that can prevent us from experiencing God's prosperity. Identifying and overcoming these obstacles is crucial:

1. Doubt and Unbelief: James 1:6-7 warns that a doubter "should not expect to receive anything from the Lord." Faith is essential for receiving God's blessings.

2. Disobedience: Sin and disobedience can hinder God's blessings. Isaiah 59:2 states, "But your iniquities have separated you from your God; your sins have hidden his face from you so that he will not hear."

3. Fear: Fear can paralyze us and prevent us from stepping into God's promises. 2 Timothy 1:7 reminds us, "For the Spirit God gave us does not make us timid, but gives us power, love and self-discipline."

4. Poverty Mindset: A poverty mindset can limit our ability to receive God's abundance. Romans 12:2 advises us to "be transformed by the renewing of your mind."

Diana Gadus, M.Ed.

Conclusion

Understanding God's will for prosperity is foundational to experiencing His blessings. God's vision of prosperity is holistic, encompassing spiritual, emotional, and physical well-being. By aligning ourselves with His will through seeking His kingdom, walking in obedience, exercising faith, practicing stewardship, cultivating generosity, and trusting in His timing, we position ourselves to receive His abundant blessings. As we continue our journey through this book, we will explore practical ways to apply these principles and overcome hindrances to prosperity, enabling us to live in the fullness of God's provision.

Diana Gadus, M.Ed.

23

Diana Gadus, M.Ed.

Chapter 4: Faith and Financial Abundance

Faith is the cornerstone of our relationship with God and plays a critical role in our financial journey. It is through faith that we unlock God's promises and experience His abundance. This chapter will delve into the relationship between faith and financial abundance, exploring biblical principles and practical applications that will help us cultivate a faith-filled approach to our finances.

The Nature of Faith

Hebrews 11:1 defines faith as "confidence in what we hope for and assurance about what we do not see." Faith involves trusting in God's promises even when we cannot see the immediate results. It requires a deep conviction that God is faithful and that His word is true.

The Role of Faith in Financial Abundance

Faith is essential for experiencing financial abundance because it aligns us with God's promises and activates His blessings. Here are several key ways in which faith influences our financial prosperity:

1. Believing in God's Provision: Philippians 4:19 assures us, "And my God will meet all your needs according to the riches of his glory in Christ Jesus." Faith involves trusting that God is our provider and that He will meet all our needs.

2. Acting on God's Promises: James 2:17 states, "In the same way, faith by itself, if it is not accompanied by action, is dead." True faith is demonstrated through action. When we believe God's promises, we take steps of faith that align with His word.

3. Speaking God's Word: Proverbs 18:21 declares, "The tongue has the power of life and death, and those who love it will eat its fruit." Faith involves speaking God's promises over our lives and finances. Our words have the power to shape our reality.

4. Overcoming Doubt and Fear: Mark 11:23-24 teaches, "Truly I tell you, if anyone says to this mountain, 'Go, throw yourself into the sea,' and does not doubt in their heart but believes that what they say will happen, it will be done for them." Faith requires overcoming doubt and fear, trusting that God will fulfill His promises.

Biblical Examples of Faith and Financial Abundance

The Bible provides numerous examples of individuals who experienced financial abundance through faith. Let us examine a few of these examples and the lessons they offer:

1. The Widow of Zarephath: In 1 Kings 17:8-16, we read the story of the widow of Zarephath. During a severe drought, God instructed the prophet Elijah to go to Zarephath, where a widow would provide for him. Despite her dire circumstances, the widow acted in faith by using her last bit of flour and oil to prepare a meal for Elijah. As a result, God miraculously provided for her, and her flour and oil did not run out.

2. The Shunammite Woman: In 2 Kings 4:8-37, the Shunammite woman demonstrated great faith by providing for the prophet Elisha. She built a room for him in her home and furnished it. In return, God blessed her with a son, and later, when her son died, Elisha raised him back to life. Her faith and generosity led to God's miraculous provision and blessings.

3. Peter and the Miraculous Catch of Fish: In Luke 5:1-11, Peter experienced a miraculous catch of fish after obeying Jesus' instruction to cast his nets into the deep water. Despite having fished all night without success, Peter acted in faith, and as a result, he caught such a large number of fish that his nets began to break.

Diana Gadus, M.Ed.

Cultivating a Faith-Filled Financial Life

To cultivate a faith-filled financial life, we must integrate faith into our financial practices. Here are some practical steps to help us do so:

1. Prayer and Seeking God's Guidance: James 1:5 encourages us to seek God's wisdom in every situation. Regular prayer and seeking God's guidance in our financial decisions are essential for aligning ourselves with His will.

2. Meditating on God's Promises: Romans 10:17 states, "Consequently, faith comes from hearing the message, and the message is heard through the word about Christ." Meditating on God's promises strengthens our faith and builds our confidence in His provision.

3. Taking Steps of Faith: Faith requires action. Identify areas where you can take steps of faith in your finances, whether it's starting a new business, investing, or giving generously. Trust that God will honor your faith and provide for your needs.

4. Declaring God's Word: Speak God's promises over your finances. Use scriptures like Philippians 4:19 and Psalm 23:1 to declare God's provision and abundance in your life.

Diana Gadus, M.Ed.

5. Trusting in God's Timing: Ecclesiastes 3:1 reminds us that "there is a time for everything, and a season for every activity under the heavens." Trust in God's timing and be patient, knowing that He will fulfill His promises at the right time.

Overcoming Challenges to Faith

Challenges to our faith are inevitable, but overcoming them is essential for experiencing God's financial abundance. Here are some common challenges and strategies for overcoming them:

1. Doubt and Unbelief: When doubt and unbelief creep in, counteract them with God's word. Meditate on scriptures that reinforce God's faithfulness and promises.

2. Fear and Anxiety: Philippians 4:6-7 advises us to "not be anxious about anything, but in every situation, by prayer and petition, with thanksgiving, present your requests to God." Replace fear and anxiety with prayer and thanksgiving.

3. Negative Influences: Surround yourself with people who encourage and support your faith journey. Avoid negative influences that sow doubt and unbelief.

4. Past Experiences: Let go of past financial failures and disappointments. Isaiah 43:18-19 encourages us to forget the former things and embrace the new things God is doing.

Diana Gadus, M.Ed.

Conclusion

Faith is a powerful force that unlocks God's promises and activates His blessings in our financial lives. By believing in God's provision, acting on His promises, speaking His word, and overcoming doubt and fear, we position ourselves to experience His financial abundance. As we cultivate a faith-filled financial life through prayer, meditation, action, declaration, and trust, we align ourselves with God's will and open the door for His miraculous provision. In the next chapter, we will explore the role of stewardship in wealth creation, further building on the foundation of faith.

Diana Gadus, M.Ed.

God Wants Me to Be Rich

Diana Gadus, M.Ed.

Chapter 5: The Role of Stewardship in Wealth Creation

Diana Gadus, M.Ed.

Stewardship is a fundamental principle in the Kingdom of God and plays a critical role in wealth creation. It involves managing God's resources wisely and responsibly, recognizing that everything we have belongs to Him. This chapter will explore the biblical concept of stewardship, its significance in wealth creation, and practical steps to become faithful stewards of God's blessings.

The Biblical Concept of Stewardship

The Bible defines stewardship as the responsible management of the resources that God has entrusted to us. This concept is rooted in the understanding that God is the ultimate owner of everything, and we are merely caretakers of His possessions. Psalm 24:1 declares, "The earth is the Lord's, and everything in it, the world, and all who live in it."

The Parable of the Talents

One of the most illustrative examples of stewardship is the Parable of the Talents found in Matthew 25:14-30. In this parable, a master entrusts his servants with varying amounts of money (talents) before going on a journey. Upon his return, he evaluates how each servant managed their entrusted resources. The servants who invested and multiplied their talents were rewarded, while the servant who did nothing with his talent was reprimanded and punished.

Diana Gadus, M.Ed.

This parable teaches several key lessons about stewardship:

1. Responsibility: Each servant was responsible for managing the master's resources. Similarly, we are responsible for managing the resources God has entrusted to us.

2. Diligence: The faithful servants took proactive steps to invest and grow their talents. Diligence and initiative are essential components of good stewardship.

3. Accountability: The master held each servant accountable for their actions. Likewise, we are accountable to God for how we manage His resources.

4. Reward: Faithful stewardship leads to increased blessings and greater responsibilities. The master rewarded the faithful servants by entrusting them with more.

Diana Gadus, M.Ed.

The Principle of Ownership

Understanding the principle of ownership is foundational to stewardship. Recognizing that God owns everything shifts our perspective from possessiveness to gratitude and responsibility. 1 Chronicles 29:11-12 states, "Yours, Lord, is the greatness and the power and the glory and the majesty and the splendor, for everything in heaven and earth is yours. Yours, Lord, is the kingdom; you are exalted as head over all. Wealth and honor come from you; you are the ruler of all things."

The Responsibilities of a Steward

As stewards, we have several key responsibilities:

1. Managing Resources Wisely: Proverbs 21:20 advises, "The wise store up choice food and olive oil, but fools gulp theirs down." Wise management involves budgeting, saving, investing, and avoiding unnecessary debt.

2. Using Resources for God's Glory: 1 Corinthians 10:31 instructs, "So whether you eat or drink or whatever you do, do it all for the glory of God." Our use of resources should reflect our commitment to God's purposes.

3. Supporting God's Work: Tithing and generous giving are essential aspects of stewardship. Malachi 3:10 encourages us to bring the whole tithe into the storehouse, promising that God will pour out abundant blessings in return.

4. Caring for Others: Stewardship includes using our resources to help those in need. Proverbs 19:17 says, "Whoever is kind to the poor lends to the Lord, and he will reward them for what they have done."

Practical Steps for Faithful Stewardship

To become faithful stewards, we must apply biblical principles to our financial practices. Here are some practical steps:

1. Create a Budget: A budget helps us manage our income and expenses effectively. Proverbs 27:23 advises, "Be sure you know the condition of your flocks, give careful attention to your herds." Keeping track of our finances ensures that we use our resources wisely.

2. Save and Invest: Saving and investing are important aspects of wealth creation. Proverbs 21:5 teaches, "The plans of the diligent lead to profit as surely as haste leads to poverty." Regular saving and prudent investments help us grow our resources.

Diana Gadus, M.Ed.

3. Avoid Debt: Debt can hinder our ability to be effective stewards. Proverbs 22:7 warns, "The rich rule over the poor, and the borrower is slave to the lender." Strive to live within your means and avoid unnecessary debt.

4. Give Generously: Generosity is a hallmark of faithful stewardship. 2 Corinthians 9:6-7 encourages us to give cheerfully and generously, promising that God will bless us abundantly.

5. Seek Financial Wisdom: Proverbs 4:7 states, "The beginning of wisdom is this: Get wisdom. Though it cost all you have, get understanding." Seek counsel and educate yourself on financial matters to make informed decisions.

6. Trust in God's Provision: Philippians 4:19 assures us, "And my God will meet all your needs according to the riches of his glory in Christ Jesus." Trusting in God's provision helps us manage resources without fear or anxiety.

Overcoming Challenges in Stewardship

Stewardship comes with its own set of challenges, but overcoming them is essential for experiencing God's blessings. Here are some common challenges and strategies to address them:

Diana Gadus, M.Ed.

1. Materialism: The desire for more can lead to poor stewardship. 1 Timothy 6:6-7 reminds us, "But godliness with contentment is great gain. For we brought nothing into the world, and we can take nothing out of it." Cultivate contentment and focus on eternal values.

2. Lack of Discipline: Managing resources requires discipline and self-control. Galatians 5:22-23 lists self-control as a fruit of the Spirit. Pray for the Holy Spirit's help to develop discipline in your financial practices.

3. Fear of Lack: Fear can prevent us from giving generously or making wise investments. Matthew 6:31-33 encourages us to seek God's kingdom first and trust that He will provide for our needs.

4. Neglecting God's Work: Focusing solely on personal gain can lead to neglecting God's work. Haggai 1:9 warns against prioritizing our own houses while neglecting God's house. Ensure that your financial priorities align with God's purposes.

Diana Gadus, M.Ed.

Conclusion

Stewardship is a vital principle in the Kingdom of God and plays a critical role in wealth creation. By understanding and embracing the biblical concept of stewardship, recognizing God's ownership, and fulfilling our responsibilities as stewards, we position ourselves to receive His blessings. Practical steps such as budgeting, saving, investing, avoiding debt, giving generously, seeking financial wisdom, and trusting in God's provision help us manage our resources effectively. As we overcome challenges and remain faithful stewards, we experience the fullness of God's prosperity. In the next chapter, we will explore the principle of tithing and how it unlocks heavenly blessings.

Chapter 6: Tithing: A Key to Unlocking Heavenly Blessings

Tithing is a principle deeply rooted in the Bible and has been a practice among God's people since ancient times. It involves giving a tenth of our income to God as an act of faith, obedience, and worship. This chapter will explore the biblical foundation of tithing, its significance, and the blessings that come from faithfully practicing this principle.

The Biblical Foundation of Tithing

The concept of tithing is first introduced in Genesis 14:18-20, where Abram (later known as Abraham) gave a tenth of everything to Melchizedek, the king of Salem and priest of God Most High. This act of giving was a response to God's blessing and a recognition of His sovereignty.

Tithing is further established in the Law of Moses. Leviticus 27:30 states, "A tithe of everything from the land, whether grain from the soil or fruit from the trees, belongs to the Lord; it is holy to the Lord." The tithe was considered holy and set apart for God.

The Purpose of Tithing

Tithing serves several important purposes in the life of a believer:

Diana Gadus, M.Ed.

God Wants Me to Be Rich

1. Acknowledging God's Ownership: Tithing is a tangible way to acknowledge that everything we have belongs to God. It is an act of surrender and recognition of His sovereignty over our lives and resources.

2. Supporting God's Work: The tithe was used to support the Levites, who were responsible for the temple services and the spiritual well-being of the community (Numbers 18:21-24). Today, tithing supports the work of the church and its ministries.

3. Building Trust and Faith: Tithing requires faith and trust in God's provision. By giving the first tenth of our income, we demonstrate our reliance on God to meet our needs.

4. Cultivating Generosity: Tithing cultivates a spirit of generosity and helps us develop a giving heart. It shifts our focus from our own needs to the needs of others and the advancement of God's kingdom.

The Promise of Blessings

The Bible contains several promises of blessings for those who faithfully tithe. One of the most well-known passages is Malachi 3:10, which states, "Bring the whole tithe into the storehouse, that there may be food in my house. Test me in this," says the Lord Almighty, "and see if I will not throw open the floodgates of heaven and pour out so much blessing that there will not be room enough to store it."

Diana Gadus, M.Ed.

This passage highlights several key points:

1. God's Challenge: God invites us to test Him in the area of tithing. This is one of the few instances in the Bible where God explicitly challenges us to test His faithfulness.

2. The Promise of Provision: God promises to pour out blessings in response to our obedience in tithing. These blessings may include financial provision, protection, and spiritual growth.

3. The Abundance of Blessings: The phrase "throw open the floodgates of heaven" indicates an overflow of blessings. God's provision is not limited; He promises abundance beyond measure.

The New Testament Perspective

While tithing is rooted in the Old Testament, the New Testament also supports the principle of giving. Jesus affirmed the practice of tithing in Matthew 23:23, where He criticized the Pharisees for neglecting justice, mercy, and faithfulness while being meticulous about tithing. Jesus' words suggest that tithing should be practiced alongside other important aspects of faith.

Diana Gadus, M.Ed.

The Apostle Paul also emphasized generous giving. In 2 Corinthians 9:6-7, he wrote, "Remember this: Whoever sows sparingly will also reap sparingly, and whoever sows generously will also reap generously. Each of you should give what you have decided in your heart to give, not reluctantly or under compulsion, for God loves a cheerful giver."

Practical Steps for Tithing

To incorporate tithing into our financial practices, we can follow these practical steps:

1. Calculate Your Tithe: Determine what constitutes a tenth of your income. This includes all sources of income, such as salary, bonuses, and other earnings.

2. Prioritize Tithing: Make tithing a priority by giving the first portion of your income to God. Proverbs 3:9 advises, "Honor the Lord with your wealth, with the firstfruits of all your crops."

3. Give Cheerfully: Approach tithing with a joyful and willing heart. 2 Corinthians 9:7 encourages us to give cheerfully, not reluctantly or under compulsion.

4. Trust in God's Provision: Have faith that God will provide for your needs as you honor Him with your tithe. Trusting in His provision strengthens our faith and deepens our relationship with Him.

Diana Gadus, M.Ed.

5. Be Consistent: Make tithing a regular practice. Consistency in tithing reflects our commitment to God and our trust in His faithfulness.

Overcoming Obstacles to Tithing

Tithing can be challenging, especially when facing financial difficulties or uncertainties. Here are some common obstacles and strategies to overcome them:

1. Fear of Lack: Fear of not having enough can hinder us from tithing. Philippians 4:19 reassures us, "And my God will meet all your needs according to the riches of his glory in Christ Jesus." Trusting in God's provision helps us overcome this fear.

2. Debt: Managing debt can make tithing seem impossible. However, prioritizing tithing can invite God's blessings and help us manage our finances more effectively. Seek financial counsel and develop a plan to pay off debt while remaining faithful in tithing.

3. Inconsistent Income: For those with irregular income, tithing can be challenging. Calculate your tithe based on each payment received, ensuring that you honor God with every increase.

4. Lack of Understanding: A lack of understanding about the importance and benefits of tithing can be an obstacle. Studying biblical teachings on tithing and seeking guidance from spiritual leaders can provide clarity and encouragement.

Conclusion

Tithing is a key principle that unlocks heavenly blessings and aligns us with God's will. It is an act of faith, obedience, and worship that acknowledges God's ownership, supports His work, builds trust, and cultivates generosity. The Bible promises abundant blessings for those who faithfully tithe, and these blessings extend beyond financial provision to include spiritual growth and protection. By incorporating tithing into our financial practices and overcoming obstacles through faith and understanding, we position ourselves to experience the fullness of God's provision. In the next chapter, we will explore the power of generosity and giving, further building on the foundation of tithing.

Diana Gadus, M.Ed.

47

Diana Gadus, M.Ed.

Chapter heading pageChapter 7: The Power of Generosity and Giving

Diana Gadus, M.Ed.

God Wants Me to Be Rich

Generosity and giving are central themes in the Bible and essential components of a prosperous life in the Kingdom of God. This chapter will explore the biblical principles of generosity, the blessings that come from giving, and practical ways to cultivate a generous heart.

The Biblical Call to Generosity

The Bible consistently calls believers to be generous and to share their blessings with others. Proverbs 11:25 states, "A generous person will prosper; whoever refreshes others will be refreshed." This verse highlights the reciprocal nature of generosity—those who give will themselves be blessed.

Jesus' Teachings on Generosity

Jesus emphasized the importance of generosity in His teachings. In Luke 6:38, He said, "Give, and it will be given to you. A good measure, pressed down, shaken together and running over, will be poured into your lap. For with the measure you use, it will be measured to you." Jesus' words encourage us to give freely, knowing that our generosity will be rewarded.

In the Parable of the Good Samaritan (Luke 10:25-37), Jesus illustrated what it means to love our neighbor through generous and selfless acts of kindness. The Samaritan's willingness to help a stranger in need exemplifies the heart of generosity that Jesus calls us to have.

Diana Gadus, M.Ed.

The Apostle Paul's Teachings on Giving

The Apostle Paul also emphasized the importance of generosity. In 2 Corinthians 9:6-7, he wrote, "Remember this: Whoever sows sparingly will also reap sparingly, and whoever sows generously will also reap generously. Each of you should give what you have decided in your heart to give, not reluctantly or under compulsion, for God loves a cheerful giver."

Paul's teachings remind us that generosity should be a deliberate and joyful act, not something done out of obligation or reluctance. Our giving should reflect the love and grace we have received from God.

The Blessings of Generosity

Generosity brings numerous blessings, both spiritual and material. Here are some of the key benefits:

1. Spiritual Growth: Generosity aligns us with God's heart and helps us grow in our faith. Acts 20:35 quotes Jesus as saying, "It is more blessed to give than to receive." Giving shifts our focus from ourselves to others, fostering spiritual maturity.

Diana Gadus, M.Ed.

2. Financial Blessings: Proverbs 3:9-10 promises, "Honor the Lord with your wealth, with the firstfruits of all your crops; then your barns will be filled to overflowing, and your vats will brim over with new wine." Generosity invites God's blessings and provision.

3. Emotional Fulfillment: Generosity brings joy and fulfillment. Acts 2:44-45 describes the early church as sharing their possessions and experiencing joy and unity. Giving to others creates a sense of purpose and satisfaction.

4. Building Relationships: Generosity strengthens relationships and fosters a sense of community. When we give to others, we build connections and demonstrate God's love in tangible ways.

5. Eternal Rewards: Matthew 6:19-21 encourages us to store up treasures in heaven by being generous on earth. Our acts of generosity have eternal significance and contribute to our heavenly rewards.

Diana Gadus, M.Ed.

Practical Ways to Cultivate Generosity

Cultivating a generous heart requires intentional effort and a willingness to be led by the Holy Spirit. Here are some practical steps to help us develop a lifestyle of generosity:

1. Recognize God's Generosity: Reflect on God's generosity towards you. John 3:16 reminds us that God gave His only Son for our salvation. Understanding the depth of God's generosity inspires us to be generous in return.

2. Start Small: Begin with small acts of generosity. Whether it's buying a meal for someone in need or donating a small amount to charity, starting small helps build the habit of giving.

3. Set Aside a Giving Fund: Create a budget that includes a designated fund for giving. Setting aside money specifically for generosity ensures that you have resources available to bless others.

4. Look for Opportunities: Be attentive to the needs around you. Ask God to open your eyes to opportunities to give and to guide you in how to help others.

Diana Gadus, M.Ed.

5. Give Your Time and Talents: Generosity is not limited to financial giving. Offer your time, skills, and talents to serve others. Volunteering and mentoring are powerful ways to give back.

6. Practice Hospitality: Open your home to others. Hospitality is a form of generosity that builds relationships and creates a welcoming environment for others.

7. Be Consistent: Make generosity a regular practice. Whether it's a monthly donation to a cause you care about or a weekly act of kindness, consistency in giving reflects a committed and generous heart.

Overcoming Barriers to Generosity

While generosity brings many blessings, there are also barriers that can hinder our willingness to give. Here are some common barriers and strategies to overcome them:

1. Fear of Not Having Enough: Fear of lack can prevent us from being generous. Philippians 4:19 assures us, "And my God will meet all your needs according to the riches of his glory in Christ Jesus." Trusting in God's provision helps us overcome this fear.

2. Selfishness: Selfishness can be a significant barrier to generosity. Romans 12:10 encourages us to "be devoted to one another in love. Honor one another above yourselves." Cultivating a selfless attitude helps us prioritize the needs of others.

Diana Gadus, M.Ed.

3. Lack of Awareness: Sometimes we are simply unaware of the needs around us. Praying for God to open our eyes and seeking opportunities to give can help us become more aware of where we can make a difference.

4. Past Experiences: Negative past experiences, such as being taken advantage of, can make us hesitant to give. Seek healing and wisdom from God, and allow Him to guide your giving decisions.

Conclusion

Generosity and giving are powerful principles that align us with God's heart and bring numerous blessings. By understanding the biblical call to generosity, recognizing the blessings that come from giving, and taking practical steps to cultivate a generous heart, we position ourselves to experience the fullness of God's provision and to make a positive impact in the lives of others. As we overcome barriers to generosity and embrace a lifestyle of giving, we reflect God's love and grace in tangible ways. In the next chapter, we will explore the role of diligence and hard work in the pursuit of wealth, further building on the principles of generosity and stewardship.

55

Diana Gadus, M.Ed.

Chapter 8: Diligence and Hard Work in Pursuit of Wealth

Diligence and hard work are essential components of wealth creation and are highly valued in the Bible. These principles not only lead to financial prosperity but also contribute to personal growth and character development. This chapter will explore the biblical perspective on diligence and hard work, their significance in the pursuit of wealth, and practical steps to cultivate these virtues.

The Biblical Perspective on Diligence and Hard Work

The Bible consistently emphasizes the importance of diligence and hard work. Proverbs 10:4 states, "Lazy hands make for poverty, but diligent hands bring wealth." This verse highlights the direct correlation between hard work and financial success.

Examples of Diligence and Hard Work in the Bible

Several biblical figures exemplify diligence and hard work in their pursuit of God's purposes:

1. Joseph: Joseph's journey from slavery to becoming the second-in-command in Egypt is a testament to his diligence and hard work. Despite facing numerous challenges, Joseph remained faithful and diligent in every task assigned to him. His hard work and integrity eventually led to his elevation and the prosperity of his family (Genesis 39-41).

2. Ruth: Ruth's dedication to her mother-in-law Naomi and her willingness to work hard in the fields demonstrate her diligence. Her efforts caught the attention of Boaz, leading to her becoming part of the lineage of King David and ultimately Jesus Christ (Ruth 2-4).

3. Nehemiah: Nehemiah's commitment to rebuilding the walls of Jerusalem showcases his diligence and leadership. Despite facing opposition, Nehemiah worked tirelessly to accomplish his mission, resulting in the successful restoration of the city's walls (Nehemiah 4:6).

The Significance of Diligence and Hard Work

Diligence and hard work are significant for several reasons:

1. Achieving Financial Prosperity: Proverbs 21:5 teaches, "The plans of the diligent lead to profit as surely as haste leads to poverty." Diligence in our work leads to financial success and stability.

2. Personal Growth and Character Development: Hard work builds character and resilience. Romans 5:3-4 states, "Not only so, but we also glory in our sufferings, because we know that suffering produces perseverance; perseverance, character; and character, hope."

Diana Gadus, M.Ed.

3. Honoring God: Colossians 3:23 encourages us to work with all our heart, as working for the Lord. Our diligence and hard work honor God and reflect our commitment to His purposes.

4. Being a Witness: Our work ethic can serve as a testimony to others. 1 Thessalonians 4:11-12 advises, "Make it your ambition to lead a quiet life: You should mind your own business and work with your hands, just as we told you, so that your daily life may win the respect of outsiders and so that you will not be dependent on anybody."

Practical Steps to Cultivate Diligence and Hard Work

Cultivating diligence and hard work requires intentional effort and discipline. Here are some practical steps to help develop these virtues:

1. Set Clear Goals: Establish clear and achievable goals for your work and personal life. Proverbs 16:3 advises, "Commit to the Lord whatever you do, and he will establish your plans." Setting goals provides direction and motivation.

2. Create a Work Plan: Develop a detailed work plan that outlines the steps needed to achieve your goals. Break down larger tasks into smaller, manageable steps to stay focused and organized.

Diana Gadus, M.Ed.

3. Prioritize Tasks: Identify and prioritize tasks based on their importance and urgency. Focus on completing high-priority tasks first to ensure that critical work is accomplished.

4. Develop a Routine: Establish a daily routine that includes dedicated time for work, rest, and personal activities. Consistency in your routine helps build discipline and productivity.

5. Stay Persistent: Perseverance is key to overcoming challenges and setbacks. Galatians 6:9 encourages us, "Let us not become weary in doing good, for at the proper time we will reap a harvest if we do not give up."

6. Seek God's Guidance: Pray for God's wisdom and guidance in your work. James 1:5 reminds us, "If any of you lacks wisdom, you should ask God, who gives generously to all without finding fault, and it will be given to you."

7. Surround Yourself with Supportive People: Surround yourself with individuals who encourage and support your efforts. Proverbs 27:17 states, "As iron sharpens iron, so one person sharpens another."

8. Take Care of Your Health: Physical and mental well-being are essential for maintaining productivity. Ensure you get enough rest, exercise regularly, and eat a balanced diet.

Overcoming Challenges to Diligence and Hard Work

Several challenges can hinder our ability to be diligent and hardworking. Here are some common challenges and strategies to overcome them:

1. Procrastination: Procrastination can delay progress and reduce productivity. Identify the root causes of procrastination and develop strategies to address them, such as breaking tasks into smaller steps or setting deadlines.

2. Distractions: Distractions can disrupt our focus and efficiency. Create a conducive work environment by minimizing distractions and setting boundaries for work and personal time.

3. Lack of Motivation: Lack of motivation can stem from various sources, including burnout or lack of interest. Revisit your goals, seek inspiration, and remind yourself of the purpose and value of your work.

4. Burnout: Overworking can lead to burnout and decreased productivity. Ensure you take regular breaks, practice self-care, and seek support when needed.

Conclusion

Diligence and hard work are essential principles for achieving financial prosperity and personal growth. By understanding the biblical perspective on these virtues and taking practical steps to cultivate them, we position ourselves for success and honor God in our work. As we overcome challenges and remain committed to our goals, we reflect the character of Christ and serve as a witness to others. In the next chapter, we will explore the role of wisdom and prudence in wealth creation, further building on the principles of diligence and hard work.

Diana Gadus, M.Ed.

Chapter 9: Wisdom and Wealth: The Role of Prudence

Diana Gadus, M.Ed.

Wisdom and prudence are crucial for successful wealth creation and management. The Bible places a high value on wisdom, often equating it with wealth and prosperity. This chapter will explore the biblical perspective on wisdom, its importance in financial matters, and practical ways to cultivate and apply wisdom and prudence in our pursuit of wealth.

The Biblical Perspective on Wisdom

The Bible frequently emphasizes the importance of wisdom. Proverbs 4:7 states, "The beginning of wisdom is this: Get wisdom. Though it cost all you have, get understanding." Wisdom is portrayed as a precious and invaluable asset that is essential for living a prosperous life.

The Relationship Between Wisdom and Wealth

Wisdom and wealth are closely linked in the Bible. Proverbs 3:13-14 says, "Blessed are those who find wisdom, those who gain understanding, for she is more profitable than silver and yields better returns than gold." This verse highlights that wisdom not only leads to financial success but is also more valuable than material riches.

Biblical Examples of Wisdom and Wealth

Several biblical figures exemplify the relationship between wisdom and wealth:

God Wants Me to Be Rich

1. Solomon: Solomon is perhaps the most well-known example of wisdom leading to wealth. When God asked Solomon what he desired, Solomon requested wisdom to govern God's people. Pleased with his request, God granted him unparalleled wisdom and also blessed him with riches and honor (1 Kings 3:5-14). Solomon's wisdom attracted wealth, prosperity, and admiration from all over the world.

2. Joseph: Joseph's wisdom and discernment enabled him to interpret Pharaoh's dreams and devise a plan to save Egypt from famine. His wise management of resources led to his promotion and the prosperity of the entire nation (Genesis 41).

3. Daniel: Daniel's wisdom and integrity earned him a high position in the Babylonian and Persian empires. His ability to interpret dreams and solve complex problems brought him favor and prosperity (Daniel 1-6).

The Importance of Prudence

Prudence is the ability to govern and discipline oneself through the use of reason. It involves careful and sensible decision-making, especially in financial matters. Proverbs 14:8 states, "The wisdom of the prudent is to give thought to their ways, but the folly of fools is deception." Prudence ensures that our decisions are well-considered and aligned with God's principles.

Diana Gadus, M.Ed.

Practical Ways to Cultivate Wisdom and Prudence

Cultivating wisdom and prudence requires intentional effort and reliance on God's guidance. Here are some practical steps:

1. Seek God's Wisdom: James 1:5 encourages us to ask God for wisdom, promising that He will give it generously. Regular prayer and seeking God's guidance in our decisions are essential for cultivating wisdom.

2. Study the Scriptures: The Bible is a rich source of wisdom. Meditating on and applying biblical principles helps us develop a godly perspective on wealth and financial management.

3. Learn from Others: Proverbs 15:22 states, "Plans fail for lack of counsel, but with many advisers they succeed." Seek advice from wise and experienced individuals, and learn from their insights and experiences.

4. Develop Critical Thinking: Cultivate the ability to think critically and analyze situations thoroughly. Proverbs 18:15 says, "The heart of the discerning acquires knowledge, for the ears of the wise seek it out."

5. Make Informed Decisions: Gather all necessary information before making financial decisions. Proverbs 19:2 warns, "Desire without knowledge is not good—how much more will hasty feet miss the way!"

Diana Gadus, M.Ed.

6. Practice Self-Discipline: Prudence involves self-discipline and the ability to delay gratification. Proverbs 25:28 teaches, "Like a city whose walls are broken through is a person who lacks self-control."

7. Reflect on Past Experiences: Learn from your past experiences, both successes and failures. Reflecting on what worked and what didn't helps you make better decisions in the future.

Applying Wisdom and Prudence in Financial Matters

Applying wisdom and prudence in financial matters involves several key practices:

1. Budgeting: Create and adhere to a budget that reflects your financial goals and priorities. A budget helps you manage your resources wisely and avoid unnecessary debt.

2. Saving and Investing: Prudently save and invest your money to build wealth over time. Proverbs 13:11 advises, "Dishonest money dwindles away, but whoever gathers money little by little makes it grow."

3. Avoiding Impulsive Decisions: Avoid making hasty financial decisions without proper consideration. Proverbs 21:5 teaches, "The plans of the diligent lead to profit as surely as haste leads to poverty."

Diana Gadus, M.Ed.

4. Diversifying Investments: Diversify your investments to manage risk and protect your wealth. Ecclesiastes 11:2 advises, "Invest in seven ventures, yes, in eight; you do not know what disaster may come upon the land."

5. Seeking Professional Advice: Consult financial advisors or professionals to make informed decisions. Their expertise can provide valuable insights and help you navigate complex financial situations.

6. Planning for the Future: Plan for future needs and contingencies, such as retirement, education, and emergencies. Proverbs 6:6-8 encourages us to learn from the ant, which stores up provisions during the harvest.

Overcoming Challenges to Wisdom and Prudence

Several challenges can hinder our ability to act with wisdom and prudence. Here are some common challenges and strategies to overcome them:

1. Emotional Decisions: Emotions can cloud our judgment and lead to poor financial decisions. Practice self-control and seek God's guidance to make decisions based on reason and wisdom.

2. Lack of Knowledge: A lack of knowledge can result in uninformed decisions. Continuously seek to expand your knowledge through reading, studying, and seeking advice.

Diana Gadus, M.Ed.

3. Peer Pressure: The influence of others can lead us to make imprudent choices. Stand firm in your convictions and seek God's approval rather than the approval of others.

4. Fear and Anxiety: Fear and anxiety can prevent us from making wise decisions. Trust in God's provision and guidance, and approach financial decisions with confidence and faith.

Conclusion

Wisdom and prudence are essential for successful wealth creation and management. By seeking God's wisdom, studying the scriptures, learning from others, and practicing self-discipline, we can cultivate these virtues and apply them to our financial decisions. As we overcome challenges and act with wisdom and prudence, we position ourselves for financial prosperity and honor God in our stewardship. In the next chapter, we will explore the concept of overcoming a poverty mindset, further building on the principles of wisdom and prudence.

Diana Gadus, M.Ed.

God Wants Me to Be Rich

Diana Gadus, M.Ed.

Chapter 10: Overcoming Poverty Mindset

Diana Gadus, M.Ed.

A poverty mindset can significantly hinder our ability to experience God's abundance and prosperity. It is a mentality characterized by a lack of belief in one's potential, fear of scarcity, and negative attitudes towards wealth and success. This chapter will explore the concept of a poverty mindset, its impact on our lives, and practical steps to overcome it and embrace God's promise of abundance.

Understanding the Poverty Mindset

A poverty mindset is not merely a lack of financial resources but a deeply ingrained belief system that influences how we view ourselves, our potential, and our relationship with money. It often manifests as:

1. Fear of Scarcity: A constant fear of not having enough, leading to hoarding, stinginess, and an inability to give generously.
2. Victim Mentality: Believing that external factors or other people are solely responsible for one's lack of success, resulting in a sense of helplessness and dependency.
3. Limiting Beliefs: Holding negative beliefs about money, wealth, and success, such as viewing wealth as inherently evil or believing that one is undeserving of prosperity.
4. Self-Sabotage: Engaging in behaviors that undermine one's financial success, such as procrastination, overspending, or avoiding opportunities for growth.

The Impact of a Poverty Mindset

A poverty mindset can have profound effects on various aspects of our lives:

1. Financial Struggles: Negative attitudes towards money and success can lead to poor financial decisions, lack of savings, and chronic debt.

2. Personal Development: A poverty mindset stifles personal growth and prevents individuals from pursuing opportunities for self-improvement and advancement.

3. Relationships: Fear of scarcity and victim mentality can strain relationships, leading to conflicts and a lack of mutual support.

4. Spiritual Life: A poverty mindset can hinder our relationship with God, as it reflects a lack of trust in His provision and abundance.

Biblical Perspective on Abundance

The Bible offers a different perspective, one of abundance and prosperity rooted in God's promises. John 10:10b says, "I have come that they may have life, and have it to the full." This verse emphasizes that Jesus came to give us an abundant life, encompassing all areas, including our finances.

Renewing the Mind

Overcoming a poverty mindset begins with renewing our minds and aligning our thoughts with God's Word. Romans 12:2 advises, "Do not conform to the pattern of this world, but be transformed by the renewing of your mind." Here are some practical steps to renew our minds:

Meditate on God's Promises: Regularly meditate on scriptures that affirm God's promises of abundance and provision. Philippians 4:19 assures us, "And my God will meet all your needs according to the riches of his glory in Christ Jesus."

Diana Gadus, M.Ed.

Replace Negative Beliefs: identify and replace limiting beliefs with positive, faith-filled affirmations. For example, replace "I will never be wealthy" with "God desires to bless me and provide for all my needs."

Practice Gratitude: Cultivate an attitude of gratitude for what you have. 1 Thessalonians 5:18 encourages us to "give thanks in all circumstances; for this is God's will for you in Christ Jesus." Gratitude shifts our focus from lack to abundance.

Seek God's Guidance: Pray for wisdom and guidance in financial matters. James 1:5 promises, "If any of you lacks wisdom, you should ask God, who gives generously to all without finding fault, and it will be given to you."

Developing a Prosperity Mindset

A prosperity mindset is grounded in faith, gratitude, and a positive outlook on life. Here are some practical steps to develop a prosperity mindset:

Set Clear Goals: Establish clear, achievable financial goals. Proverbs 21:5 teaches, "The plans of the diligent lead to profit as surely as haste leads to poverty."

Diana Gadus, M.Ed.

Invest in Personal Growth: Continuously seek opportunities for learning and self-improvement. Proverbs 4:7 advises, "The beginning of wisdom is this: Get wisdom. Though it cost all you have, get understanding."

Surround Yourself with Positive Influences: Associate with people who inspire and encourage you to pursue your goals. Proverbs 27:17 states, "As iron sharpens iron, so one person sharpens another."

Practice Generosity: Generosity is a powerful antidote to a poverty mindset. Proverbs 11:25 says, "A generous person will prosper; whoever refreshes others will be refreshed." Giving opens the door to God's blessings and shifts our focus from scarcity to abundance.

Embrace Opportunities: Be willing to take risks and embrace new opportunities for growth and advancement. Matthew 25:14-30, the Parable of the Talents, encourages us to use our gifts and opportunities wisely.

Trust in God's Provision: Develop a deep trust in God's ability to provide for your needs. Matthew 6:31-33 reminds us, "So do not worry, saying, 'What shall we eat?' or 'What shall we drink?' or 'What shall we wear?' For the pagans run after all these things, and your heavenly Father knows that you need them. But seek first his kingdom and his righteousness, and all these things will be given to you as well."

Diana Gadus, M.Ed.

Overcoming Challenges to a Prosperity Mindset

Transitioning from a poverty mindset to a prosperity mindset may present challenges. Here are some common challenges and strategies to overcome them:

1. Fear of Failure: Fear of failure can prevent us from pursuing opportunities. 2 Timothy 1:7 encourages us, "For the Spirit God gave us does not make us timid, but gives us power, love and self-discipline." Embrace failure as a learning experience and a stepping stone to success.
2. Past Experiences: Negative past experiences can shape our beliefs and attitudes. Philippians 3:13-14 advises us to forget what is behind and strive toward what is ahead. Let go of past failures and focus on God's promises for the future.
3. Comparison: Comparing ourselves to others can lead to dissatisfaction and a sense of lack. Galatians 6:4-5 encourages us to take pride in our own achievements without comparing ourselves to others. Focus on your unique journey and progress.

Conclusion

Diana Gadus, M.Ed.

God Wants Me to Be Rich

Overcoming a poverty mindset is essential for experiencing God's abundance and prosperity. By renewing our minds with God's Word, developing a prosperity mindset, and overcoming challenges through faith and trust in God's provision, we position ourselves to receive His blessings. As we embrace a positive outlook and take practical steps towards financial growth, we reflect God's goodness and demonstrate His provision in our lives. In the next chapter, we will explore the concept of aligning our financial goals with God's purpose, further building on the principles of overcoming a poverty mindset.

Diana Gadus, M.Ed.

Chapter 11: Wealth and Purpose: Aligning Financial Goals with God's Plan

God Wants Me to Be Rich

Aligning our financial goals with God's purpose is crucial for experiencing true prosperity and fulfillment. When our financial pursuits are in harmony with God's plan, we not only achieve personal success but also contribute to the advancement of His kingdom. This chapter will explore the importance of aligning our financial goals with God's purpose, practical steps to achieve this alignment, and the blessings that come from living a purpose-driven financial life.

The Importance of Aligning Financial Goals with God's Purpose

Aligning our financial goals with God's purpose ensures that our pursuits are meaningful and impactful. Here are some key reasons why this alignment is important:

Fulfillment: True fulfillment comes from living a life that aligns with God's purpose. Ephesians 2:10 reminds us, "For we are God's handiwork, created in Christ Jesus to do good works, which God prepared in advance for us to do." When our financial goals reflect God's plan, we experience a deeper sense of satisfaction and fulfillment.

Kingdom Impact: Our financial resources can significantly impact the advancement of God's kingdom. Matthew 6:19-21 encourages us to store up treasures in heaven by using our resources for eternal purposes. Aligning our financial goals with God's plan allows us to contribute to ministries, missions, and charitable causes that further His work.

Diana Gadus, M.Ed.

Stewardship: Recognizing that everything we have belongs to God, we are called to be faithful stewards of His resources. 1 Peter 4:10 advises, "Each of you should use whatever gift you have received to serve others, as faithful stewards of God's grace in its various forms." Aligning our financial goals with God's purpose ensures that we manage His resources wisely and responsibly.

Blessings: When we prioritize God's purposes, He promises to bless us abundantly. Proverbs 3:9-10 states, "Honor the Lord with your wealth, with the firstfruits of all your crops; then your barns will be filled to overflowing, and your vats will brim over with new wine." Aligning our financial goals with God's plan positions us to receive His blessings.

Practical Steps to Align Financial Goals with God's Purpose

To align our financial goals with God's purpose, we must be intentional and seek His guidance. Here are some practical steps to achieve this alignment:

Seek God's Guidance: Begin by seeking God's guidance through prayer and meditation. James 1:5 encourages us to ask God for wisdom, promising that He will give it generously. Ask God to reveal His purpose for your life and to guide your financial decisions.

Diana Gadus, M.Ed.

Identify Your Calling: Reflect on your unique gifts, talents, and passions. Consider how these can be used to serve God's purposes. Ephesians 4:1 urges us to "live a life worthy of the calling you have received." Align your financial goals with your calling and use your resources to further your God-given mission.

Set Purpose-Driven Goals: Establish financial goals that reflect your commitment to God's purposes. Whether it's supporting a specific ministry, funding a mission trip, or giving to charitable causes, ensure that your goals align with your desire to advance God's kingdom.

Create a Budget: Develop a budget that prioritizes God's purposes. Allocate a portion of your income to tithing, giving, and supporting causes that align with God's plan. Proverbs 21:5 teaches, "The plans of the diligent lead to profit as surely as haste leads to poverty." A budget helps you manage your resources effectively and stay focused on your goals.

Invest in Eternal Impact: Consider how your investments can have an eternal impact. Look for opportunities to invest in businesses, projects, or organizations that align with your values and God's purposes. Matthew 6:33 reminds us to seek first God's kingdom and His righteousness, trusting that all other things will be added to us.

Diana Gadus, M.Ed.

Regularly Review and Adjust: Periodically review your financial goals and assess whether they continue to align with God's purpose. Be open to making adjustments as God leads. Proverbs 16:9 states, "In their hearts humans plan their course, but the Lord establishes their steps." Allow God to direct your financial path.

The Blessings of Living a Purpose-Driven Financial Life

Living a purpose-driven financial life brings numerous blessings:

Peace and Contentment: Aligning our financial goals with God's purpose brings peace and contentment. Philippians 4:11-12 teaches us to be content in all circumstances, trusting that God will provide for our needs.

Joy of Giving: There is great joy in giving and contributing to God's work. Acts 20:35 quotes Jesus as saying, "It is more blessed to give than to receive." Generosity brings joy and fulfillment.

Increased Provision: When we prioritize God's purposes, He promises to provide for our needs abundantly. 2 Corinthians 9:8 assures us, "And God is able to bless you abundantly, so that in all things at all times, having all that you need, you will abound in every good work."

Diana Gadus, M.Ed.

Eternal Rewards: Our investments in God's kingdom have eternal significance. Matthew 6:20 encourages us to "store up for yourselves treasures in heaven, where moths and vermin do not destroy, and where thieves do not break in and steal."

Overcoming Challenges to Aligning Financial Goals with God's Purpose

Aligning our financial goals with God's purpose may present challenges. Here are some common challenges and strategies to overcome them:

Worldly Pressures: The pressure to conform to worldly standards of success can be overwhelming. Romans 12:2 advises, "Do not conform to the pattern of this world, but be transformed by the renewing of your mind." Focus on God's standards and seek His approval.

Fear of Insufficiency: Fear of not having enough can hinder our willingness to prioritize God's purposes. Matthew 6:31-33 reminds us to trust in God's provision and to seek His kingdom first.

Distractions: Distractions and competing priorities can divert our attention from God's purposes. Hebrews 12:1 encourages us to "throw off everything that hinders and the sin that so easily entangles" and to "run with perseverance the race marked out for us."

Diana Gadus, M.Ed.

Lack of Clarity: Uncertainty about God's purpose can make it challenging to set aligned financial goals. Seek God's guidance through prayer, study, and counsel from trusted spiritual leaders.

Conclusion

Aligning our financial goals with God's purpose is essential for experiencing true prosperity and fulfillment. By seeking God's guidance, identifying our calling, setting purpose-driven goals, creating a budget, investing in eternal impact, and regularly reviewing our goals, we position ourselves to live a purpose-driven financial life. The blessings of peace, contentment, joy, increased provision, and eternal rewards await those who prioritize God's purposes in their financial pursuits. In the next chapter, we will explore the principles of ethical wealth building, further building on the foundation of aligning our financial goals with God's purpose.

87

Diana Gadus, M.Ed.

Chapter 12: Ethical Wealth Building: Honesty and Integrity

Ethical wealth building is crucial for sustainable prosperity and reflects our commitment to living according to God's principles. Honesty and integrity are foundational to ethical wealth building and are essential for maintaining a clear conscience and a positive testimony. This chapter will explore the importance of honesty and integrity in wealth building, practical steps to maintain ethical standards, and the blessings that come from living a life of integrity.

The Importance of Honesty and Integrity

Honesty and integrity are highly valued in the Bible and are essential for ethical wealth building. Proverbs 11:1 states, "The Lord detests dishonest scales, but accurate weights find favor with him." This verse emphasizes that God values honesty and integrity in all our dealings.

Biblical Examples of Honesty and Integrity

Several biblical figures exemplify the importance of honesty and integrity:

Joseph: Joseph's unwavering integrity earned him favor and success in Egypt. Despite being falsely accused and imprisoned, Joseph maintained his integrity and was eventually promoted to a position of great authority (Genesis 39-41).

Daniel: Daniel's commitment to honesty and integrity set him apart in the Babylonian and Persian empires. His refusal to compromise his principles earned him the respect of kings and a prominent position in the government (Daniel 1-6).

Nehemiah: Nehemiah's integrity and dedication to rebuilding the walls of Jerusalem inspired trust and support from the people. His ethical leadership ensured the successful completion of the project (Nehemiah 4:6).

The Role of Honesty and Integrity in Wealth Building

Honesty and integrity play a crucial role in wealth building for several reasons:

1. Trust: Trust is the foundation of all successful relationships, including business relationships. Proverbs 22:1 teaches, "A good name is more desirable than great riches; to be esteemed is better than silver or gold." Maintaining honesty and integrity builds trust with clients, partners, and colleagues.

2. Sustainability: Ethical wealth building ensures long-term success. Proverbs 10:9 states, "Whoever walks in integrity walks securely, but whoever takes crooked paths will be found out." Dishonest practices may bring temporary gains but ultimately lead to ruin.

Diana Gadus, M.Ed.

3. Blessings: God promises to bless those who walk in integrity. Psalm 84:11 says, "For the Lord God is a sun and shield; the Lord bestows favor and honor; no good thing does he withhold from those whose walk is blameless." Living a life of integrity invites God's favor and blessings.

Practical Steps to Maintain Honesty and Integrity

Maintaining honesty and integrity requires intentional effort and commitment. Here are some practical steps to uphold ethical standards:

1. Set Clear Ethical Standards: Establish clear ethical guidelines for yourself and your business. Proverbs 16:3 advises, "Commit to the Lord whatever you do, and he will establish your plans." Ensure that your standards align with biblical principles.

2. Be Transparent: Practice transparency in all your dealings. Proverbs 12:22 states, "The Lord detests lying lips, but he delights in people who are trustworthy." Be open and honest with clients, partners, and colleagues.

3. Honor Your Commitments: Follow through on your promises and commitments. Psalm 15:4 describes a person of integrity as one "who keeps an oath even when it hurts, and does not change their mind."

Diana Gadus, M.Ed.

4. Avoid Deceptive Practices: Refrain from engaging in deceptive or manipulative practices. Proverbs 20:23 warns, "The Lord detests differing weights, and dishonest scales do not please him." Ensure that your business practices are fair and just.

5. Seek Accountability: Surround yourself with trusted individuals who can hold you accountable. Proverbs 27:17 states, "As iron sharpens iron, so one person sharpens another." Accountability helps maintain integrity and ethical standards.

6. Reflect on Your Actions: Regularly reflect on your actions and decisions to ensure they align with your ethical standards. Psalm 139:23-24 invites God to search our hearts and reveal any wrongdoing: "Search me, God, and know my heart; test me and know my anxious thoughts. See if there is any offensive way in me, and lead me in the way everlasting."

The Blessings of Living a Life of Integrity

Living a life of integrity brings numerous blessings:

1. Peace of Mind: Honesty and integrity provide peace of mind and a clear conscience. Proverbs 28:1 teaches, "The wicked flee though no one pursues, but the righteous are as bold as a lion."

Diana Gadus, M.Ed.

2. Positive Reputation: Integrity builds a positive reputation and earns the respect of others. Proverbs 31:10-11 praises the virtuous woman whose husband has full confidence in her and lacks nothing of value.

3. God's Favor: God promises to bless those who walk in integrity. Psalm 25:21 declares, "May integrity and uprightness protect me, because my hope, Lord, is in you."

4. Long-Term Success: Ethical wealth building ensures sustainable and long-term success. Proverbs 13:11 states, "Dishonest money dwindles away, but whoever gathers money little by little makes it grow."

Overcoming Challenges to Honesty and Integrity

Maintaining honesty and integrity can be challenging, especially in a world that often prioritizes success over ethics. Here are some common challenges and strategies to overcome them:

1. Pressure to Compromise: The pressure to compromise ethical standards for financial gain can be strong. Romans 12:2 advises, "Do not conform to the pattern of this world, but be transformed by the renewing of your mind." Stay committed to God's principles and trust in His provision.

Diana Gadus, M.Ed.

2. Temptation: Temptation to engage in dishonest practices can arise in various forms. 1 Corinthians 10:13 assures us that God provides a way out of every temptation. Seek God's strength to resist and make ethical choices.

3. Fear of Loss: Fear of financial loss can lead to unethical decisions. Matthew 6:31-33 reminds us to trust in God's provision and to seek His kingdom first. Trust that God will honor your integrity and provide for your needs.

4. Negative Influences: Negative influences from peers or the business environment can challenge your commitment to integrity. Proverbs 13:20 advises, "Walk with the wise and become wise, for a companion of fools suffers harm." Surround yourself with positive influences who uphold similar ethical standards.

Diana Gadus, M.Ed.

Conclusion

Ethical wealth building, grounded in honesty and integrity, is essential for sustainable prosperity and a positive testimony. By setting clear ethical standards, practicing transparency, honoring commitments, avoiding deceptive practices, seeking accountability, and reflecting on our actions, we maintain integrity in all our dealings. The blessings of peace of mind, a positive reputation, God's favor, and long-term success await those who live a life of integrity. As we overcome challenges and stay committed to ethical principles, we honor God and reflect His character in our wealth-building endeavors. In the next chapter, we will explore principles of managing wealth God's way, further building on the foundation of ethical wealth building.

Diana Gadus, M.Ed.

Chapter 13: Managing Wealth God's Way: Financial Planning and Management

Managing wealth according to God's principles is crucial for achieving sustainable prosperity and fulfilling His purposes in our lives. Effective financial planning and management involve using our resources wisely, making informed decisions, and aligning our financial practices with biblical teachings. This chapter will explore principles of managing wealth God's way, practical steps for financial planning and management, and the blessings that come from honoring God with our resources.

The Biblical Foundation of Financial Management

The Bible provides comprehensive guidance on financial management, emphasizing the importance of wisdom, diligence, and stewardship. Proverbs 21:5 states, "The plans of the diligent lead to profit as surely as haste leads to poverty." This verse highlights the value of careful planning and diligent effort in achieving financial success.

Principles of Managing Wealth God's Way

Managing wealth God's way involves several key principles:

1. Stewardship: Recognize that everything we have belongs to God, and we are stewards of His resources. 1 Peter 4:10 advises, "Each of you should use whatever gift you have received to serve others, as faithful stewards of God's grace in its various forms."

2. Wisdom: Seek God's wisdom in all financial matters.

Principles of Managing Wealth God's Way

Managing wealth God's way involves several key principles:

1. Stewardship: Recognize that everything we have belongs to God, and we are stewards of His resources. 1 Peter 4:10 advises, "Each of you should use whatever gift you have received to serve others, as faithful stewards of God's grace in its various forms."

2. Wisdom: Seek God's wisdom in all financial matters. James 1:5 encourages, "If any of you lacks wisdom, you should ask God, who gives generously to all without finding fault, and it will be given to you." God's wisdom helps us make sound financial decisions.

3. Planning: Proverbs 21:5 emphasizes the importance of planning, "The plans of the diligent lead to profit as surely as haste leads to poverty." Effective planning involves setting goals, creating budgets, and preparing for future needs.

4. Contentment: Philippians 4:11-12 teaches the value of contentment, "I have learned to be content whatever the circumstances. I know what it is to be in need, and I know what it is to have plenty." Contentment helps us avoid the pitfalls of greed and unnecessary debt.

Diana Gadus, M.Ed.

5. Generosity: Practicing generosity aligns with God's heart. Proverbs 11:25 states, "A generous person will prosper; whoever refreshes others will be refreshed." Generosity ensures we use our resources to bless others and advance God's kingdom.

6. Integrity: Honesty and integrity are crucial in financial dealings. Proverbs 10:9 teaches, "Whoever walks in integrity walks securely, but whoever takes crooked paths will be found out." Integrity builds trust and ensures long-term success.

Practical Steps for Financial Planning and Management

Implementing these principles requires practical steps and disciplined effort. Here are some steps to help you manage your wealth God's way:

1. Create a Budget: Develop a budget that outlines your income, expenses, savings, and giving. Ensure that your budget reflects your financial goals and priorities. Proverbs 27:23-24 advises, "Be sure you know the condition of your flocks, give careful attention to your herds; for riches do not endure forever, and a crown is not secure for all generations."

2. Set Financial Goals: Establish clear and achievable financial goals. Whether it's saving for retirement, funding education, or supporting a ministry, set goals that align with God's purposes for your life.

Diana Gadus, M.Ed.

3. Save and Invest Wisely: Proverbs 21:20 highlights the importance of saving, "The wise store up choice food and olive oil, but fools gulp theirs down." Save regularly and invest wisely to build wealth over time. Diversify your investments to manage risk and seek professional advice when necessary.

4. Avoid Debt: Proverbs 22:7 warns, "The rich rule over the poor, and the borrower is slave to the lender." Avoid unnecessary debt and strive to live within your means. If you have existing debt, develop a plan to pay it off systematically.

5. Give Generously: Incorporate giving into your financial plan. Set aside a portion of your income for tithing and charitable contributions. 2 Corinthians 9:6-7 encourages cheerful giving, "Remember this: Whoever sows sparingly will also reap sparingly, and whoever sows generously will also reap generously. Each of you should give what you have decided in your heart to give, not reluctantly or under compulsion, for God loves a cheerful giver."

6. Prepare for Emergencies: Build an emergency fund to cover unexpected expenses. Having a financial cushion helps you navigate crises without derailing your long-term goals. Proverbs 22:3 states, "The prudent see danger and take refuge, but the simple keep going and pay the penalty."

Diana Gadus, M.Ed.

7. Seek Professional Advice: Consult with financial advisors or experts to make informed decisions. Proverbs 15:22 advises, "Plans fail for lack of counsel, but with many advisers they succeed." Professional advice can provide valuable insights and help you achieve your financial goals.

The Blessings of Honoring God with Our Resources

When we manage our wealth according to God's principles, we invite His blessings into our lives. Here are some of the blessings that come from honoring God with our resources:

1. Peace of Mind: Effective financial management brings peace of mind and reduces stress. Knowing that you are managing your resources wisely and in alignment with God's will provides a sense of security and contentment.

2. Financial Stability: Adhering to biblical principles of financial management leads to greater financial stability and prosperity. Proverbs 10:22 states, "The blessing of the Lord brings wealth, without painful toil for it."

3. Joy of Giving: Generosity brings joy and fulfillment. Acts 20:35 quotes Jesus, "It is more blessed to give than to receive." Giving to others and supporting God's work enriches our lives and strengthens our faith.

Diana Gadus, M.Ed.

4. Positive Testimony: Managing our wealth with integrity and wisdom serves as a powerful testimony to others. It reflects God's character and can inspire others to seek His guidance in their financial matters.

5. Eternal Rewards: Our investments in God's kingdom have eternal significance. Matthew 6:20 encourages, "But store up for yourselves treasures in heaven, where moths and vermin do not destroy, and where thieves do not break in and steal."

Overcoming Challenges in Financial Management

Managing wealth according to God's principles can present challenges, but with faith and diligence, these can be overcome. Here are some common challenges and strategies to address them:

1. Impulsive Spending: Impulsive spending can derail your financial plan. Practice self-control and discipline. Proverbs 25:28 advises, "Like a city whose walls are broken through is a person who lacks self-control."

2. Lack of Knowledge: A lack of financial knowledge can lead to poor decisions. Continuously educate yourself on financial matters through reading, courses, and seeking advice from experts.

3. Fear of Risk: Fear of risk can prevent you from making wise investments. Seek God's guidance and wise counsel to make informed decisions. Proverbs 3:5-6 encourages, "Trust in the Lord with all your heart and lean not on your own understanding; in all your ways submit to him, and he will make your paths straight."

4. Inconsistent Income: Managing finances with inconsistent income can be challenging. Create a flexible budget and prioritize essential expenses. Save diligently during periods of higher income to cover leaner times.

Conclusion

Managing wealth according to God's principles involves stewardship, wisdom, planning, contentment, generosity, and integrity. By implementing practical steps such as creating a budget, setting financial goals, saving and investing wisely, avoiding debt, giving generously, preparing for emergencies, and seeking professional advice, we honor God with our resources and position ourselves for His blessings. Overcoming challenges through faith, discipline, and continuous learning ensures long-term success and fulfillment. As we continue our journey, the next chapter will explore the spiritual warfare and wealth, providing insights on overcoming obstacles that hinder our financial prosperity.

Diana Gadus, M.Ed.

Chapter 14: Spiritual Warfare and Wealth: Overcoming Obstacles

In the journey toward financial prosperity, believers may encounter spiritual obstacles that hinder their progress. Recognizing and overcoming these obstacles is crucial for experiencing the fullness of God's blessings. This chapter will explore the concept of spiritual warfare in the context of wealth, identify common spiritual obstacles, and provide strategies for overcoming them through faith and God's Word.

Understanding Spiritual Warfare

Spiritual warfare refers to the battle between the forces of good and evil, which affects various aspects of our lives, including our finances. Ephesians 6:12 reminds us, "For our struggle is not against flesh and blood, but against the rulers, against the authorities, against the powers of this dark world and against the spiritual forces of evil in the heavenly realms." Understanding this battle helps us recognize the spiritual dimensions of financial challenges.

Common Spiritual Obstacles to Wealth

Several spiritual obstacles can hinder our financial prosperity. Here are some of the most common:

1. Fear and Anxiety: Fear of financial instability and anxiety about the future can paralyze us and prevent us from taking necessary steps toward financial growth. Philippians 4:6-7 encourages, "Do not be anxious about anything, but in every situation, by prayer and petition, with thanksgiving, present your requests to God. And the peace of God, which transcends all understanding, will guard your hearts and your minds in Christ Jesus."

2. Greed and Materialism: An excessive focus on accumulating wealth for selfish purposes can lead to greed and materialism, which are contrary to God's principles. 1 Timothy 6:10 warns, "For the love of money is a root of all kinds of evil. Some people, eager for money, have wandered from the faith and pierced themselves with many griefs."

3. Pride and Self-Reliance: Relying solely on our abilities and pridefully seeking wealth can lead to a fall. Proverbs 16:18 states, "Pride goes before destruction, a haughty spirit before a fall." Humility and dependence on God are essential for true prosperity.

4. Spiritual Oppression: Spiritual oppression can manifest as persistent financial difficulties, blockages, or attacks that hinder financial progress. James 4:7 advises, "Submit yourselves, then, to God. Resist the devil, and he will flee from you."

Diana Gadus, M.Ed.

Strategies for Overcoming Spiritual Obstacles

Overcoming spiritual obstacles requires faith, prayer, and the application of God's Word. Here are strategies to help you overcome these challenges:

1. Prayer and Fasting: Engage in prayer and fasting to seek God's guidance and break spiritual strongholds. Matthew 17:21 emphasizes the power of prayer and fasting, "But this kind does not go out except by prayer and fasting."

2. Renewing the Mind: Renew your mind with God's Word to overcome fear, anxiety, and negative thinking. Romans 12:2 instructs, "Do not conform to the pattern of this world, but be transformed by the renewing of your mind." Meditate on scriptures that affirm God's promises of provision and abundance.

3. Generosity: Combat greed and materialism by practicing generosity. Acts 20:35 quotes Jesus, "It is more blessed to give than to receive." Generosity shifts our focus from accumulating wealth to blessing others and advancing God's kingdom.

4. Humility and Dependence on God: Cultivate humility and acknowledge your dependence on God for financial success. Proverbs 3:5-6 advises, "Trust in the Lord with all your heart and lean not on your own understanding; in all your ways submit to him, and he will make your paths straight."

Diana Gadus, M.Ed.

5. Spiritual Warfare Prayers: Pray specific prayers to resist the enemy's attacks and claim God's promises. Ephesians 6:10-18 describes the armor of God, which equips us for spiritual warfare. Pray these scriptures to stand firm against spiritual obstacles.

6. Seeking Godly Counsel: Seek counsel from trusted spiritual leaders and mentors who can provide guidance and support. Proverbs 15:22 states, "Plans fail for lack of counsel, but with many advisers they succeed."

Applying Biblical Principles in Financial Decisions

Applying biblical principles in your financial decisions is crucial for overcoming spiritual obstacles. Here are some practical steps:

Tithing and Offerings: Honor God with your tithes and offerings. Malachi 3:10 promises, "Bring the whole tithe into the storehouse, that there may be food in my house. Test me in this," says the Lord Almighty, "and see if I will not throw open the floodgates of heaven and pour out so much blessing that there will not be room enough to store it."

Debt Management: Avoid excessive debt and strive to live within your means. Proverbs 22:7 warns, "The rich rule over the poor, and the borrower is slave to the lender." Develop a plan to pay off existing debt and avoid incurring new debt.

Diana Gadus, M.Ed.

God Wants Me to Be Rich

Wise Investments: Make informed and prudent investment decisions. Ecclesiastes 11:2 advises, "Invest in seven ventures, yes, in eight; you do not know what disaster may come upon the land." Diversify your investments to manage risk.

Savings and Emergency Fund: Build a savings and emergency fund to cover unexpected expenses. Proverbs 21:20 highlights the importance of saving, "The wise store up choice food and olive oil, but fools gulp theirs down."

Testimonies of God's Provision

Sharing testimonies of God's provision can inspire faith and encourage others. Here are some examples:

George Müller: George Müller, a Christian evangelist and director of the Ashley Down orphanage in Bristol, England, trusted God for financial provision. Through prayer and faith, he provided for thousands of orphans without ever soliciting donations. Müller's testimony is a powerful example of God's faithfulness.

John Wesley: John Wesley, the founder of the Methodist movement, practiced and preached financial stewardship. Despite earning a substantial income from his writings, he lived frugally and gave generously. Wesley's life exemplifies the principles of generosity and dependence on God.

Diana Gadus, M.Ed.

R.G. LeTourneau: R.G. LeTourneau, an industrialist and inventor, attributed his financial success to his commitment to tithing and generous giving. He gave away 90% of his income and lived on the remaining 10%, demonstrating that God's blessings follow faithful stewardship.

Conclusion

Overcoming spiritual obstacles to wealth requires recognizing the spiritual dimensions of financial challenges and applying biblical principles to our financial decisions. By engaging in prayer and fasting, renewing our minds, practicing generosity, cultivating humility, praying spiritual warfare prayers, and seeking godly counsel, we can overcome these obstacles and experience God's provision. Testimonies of God's faithfulness serve as powerful reminders of His ability to provide abundantly. As we continue our journey, the next chapter will explore the concept of living in abundance and sharing testimonies of God's provision, further building on the principles of spiritual warfare and wealth.

Diana Gadus, M.Ed.

God Wants Me to Be Rich

Diana Gadus, M.Ed.

Chapter 15: Living in Abundance: Testimonies of God's Provision

Living in abundance is about experiencing the fullness of God's blessings in every area of our lives. It is a testament to His faithfulness, provision, and the fulfillment of His promises. This chapter will explore what it means to live in abundance, share testimonies of God's provision, and provide practical steps to maintain a life of abundance and gratitude.

Understanding Abundance

Abundance in the biblical sense goes beyond material wealth. It encompasses spiritual, emotional, and physical well-being. John 10:10b states, "I have come that they may have life, and have it to the full." Living in abundance means experiencing the richness of life that Jesus came to offer.

Testimonies of God's Provision

Sharing testimonies of God's provision encourages faith and inspires others to trust in His promises. Here are some powerful examples:

1. The Widow of Zarephath: In 1 Kings 17:8-16, God provided for the widow of Zarephath during a severe drought. Despite her meager resources, she obeyed Elijah's request to bake him a loaf of bread. In return, God ensured her jar of flour and jug of oil never ran dry until the drought ended. This story demonstrates God's miraculous provision and the blessings of obedience.

2. The Feeding of the 5,000: In Matthew 14:13-21, Jesus fed 5,000 people with five loaves of bread and two fish. After everyone had eaten, the disciples collected twelve baskets of leftovers. This miracle illustrates God's ability to multiply our resources and provide abundantly.

3. Corrie ten Boom: Corrie ten Boom, a Dutch Christian who helped many Jews escape the Nazis during World War II, often experienced God's provision. Despite limited resources, she trusted God to supply her needs. Her autobiography, "The Hiding Place," is filled with testimonies of God's faithfulness and provision.

Living in Abundance

Living in abundance involves several key practices:

Diana Gadus, M.Ed.

God Wants Me to Be Rich

1. Gratitude: Cultivate an attitude of gratitude for God's blessings. 1 Thessalonians 5:18 encourages, "Give thanks in all circumstances; for this is God's will for you in Christ Jesus." Gratitude shifts our focus from what we lack to what we have.

2. Generosity: Continue practicing generosity, recognizing that it invites God's blessings. Proverbs 11:25 states, "A generous person will prosper; whoever refreshes others will be refreshed." Generosity reflects God's heart and opens the door to further blessings.

3. Faith and Trust: Maintain faith and trust in God's provision. Philippians 4:19 assures, "And my God will meet all your needs according to the riches of his glory in Christ Jesus." Trusting in God's faithfulness provides peace and security.

4. Wise Stewardship: Manage your resources wisely and responsibly. Proverbs

5. Contentment: Embrace contentment in every situation. Hebrews 13:5 advises, "Keep your lives free from the love of money and be content with what you have, because God has said, 'Never will I leave you; never will I forsake you.'" Contentment guards against greed and dissatisfaction.

Diana Gadus, M.Ed.

6. Purposeful Living: Align your life with God's purposes. Matthew 6:33 encourages, "But seek first his kingdom and his righteousness, and all these things will be given to you as well." When our lives and finances align with God's purposes, we experience true abundance.

Practical Steps to Maintain a Life of Abundance

To live a life of abundance, implement these practical steps:

1. Regular Reflection: Take time to regularly reflect on God's blessings and provision in your life. Keeping a gratitude journal can help you focus on and remember His faithfulness.

2. Balanced Living: Maintain a balanced approach to life, including work, rest, relationships, and spiritual growth. Balance ensures that you do not become overwhelmed by any single aspect of life.

3. Continuous Learning: Invest in continuous learning and personal development. Proverbs 4:7 teaches, "The beginning of wisdom is this: Get wisdom. Though it cost all you have, get understanding." Knowledge and wisdom contribute to making informed and effective decisions.

Diana Gadus, M.Ed.

4. Community Engagement: Engage with your community and build supportive relationships. Acts 2:44-45 describes the early church's communal living and generosity, which fostered a strong sense of unity and support.

5. Health and Well-being: Prioritize your physical, emotional, and spiritual health. 3 John 1:2 expresses the desire for overall well-being, "Dear friend, I pray that you may enjoy good health and that all may go well with you, even as your soul is getting along well."

6. Prayer and Devotion: Maintain a strong prayer and devotional life. Philippians 4:6-7 emphasizes the importance of prayer, "Do not be anxious about anything, but in every situation, by prayer and petition, with thanksgiving, present your requests to God. And the peace of God, which transcends all understanding, will guard your hearts and your minds in Christ Jesus."

Testimonies of Abundant Living

Hearing testimonies of those who have experienced God's abundant provision can inspire and encourage us. Here are a few more powerful examples:

Diana Gadus, M.Ed.

1. David Green: David Green, the founder of Hobby Lobby, attributes his company's success to his commitment to biblical principles, including generosity and tithing. Despite financial challenges, his faithfulness has led to remarkable growth and impact.

2. J.C. Penney: James Cash Penney, the founder of the J.C. Penney stores, began his business with a commitment to the Golden Rule and biblical principles of integrity and fairness. His commitment to these values contributed to his business success and enduring legacy.

3. Mary Kay Ash: Mary Kay Ash, founder of Mary Kay Cosmetics, built her company on principles of faith and generosity. Her emphasis on empowering others and giving back has led to a thriving global enterprise that continues to impact lives positively.

Embracing God's Promise of Abundance

Embracing God's promise of abundance involves believing in His desire to bless us and living in a way that honors Him. Deuteronomy 28:11-12 promises, "The Lord will grant you abundant prosperity—in the fruit of your womb, the young of your livestock and the crops of your ground—in the land he swore to your ancestors to give you. The Lord will open the heavens, the storehouse of his bounty, to send rain on your land in season and to bless all the work of your hands."

Diana Gadus, M.Ed.

Conclusion

Living in abundance is about experiencing the fullness of God's blessings in every area of our lives. By practicing gratitude, generosity, faith, wise stewardship, contentment, and purposeful living, we align ourselves with God's principles and invite His blessings. Practical steps such as regular reflection, balanced living, continuous learning, community engagement, prioritizing health and well-being, and maintaining a strong prayer life help us sustain a life of abundance.

Testimonies of God's provision serve as powerful reminders of His faithfulness and ability to provide abundantly. As we embrace God's promise of abundance, we reflect His goodness and serve as a testament to His love and provision. By living a life of abundance, we not only experience personal fulfillment but also contribute to the advancement of God's kingdom and the well-being of others.

Diana Gadus, M.Ed.

Epilogue: A Reflection on God's Abundant Provision

As we come to the conclusion of this journey, it is essential to pause and reflect on the profound truths we've explored together. The idea that God desires for us to live in abundance and prosperity, though perhaps initially surprising to some, is deeply rooted in Scripture and the very nature of God Himself. Throughout this book, we have delved into the biblical principles that guide us toward wealth and prosperity, not as an end in themselves, but as a means to fulfill God's purposes in our lives and the lives of those around us.

The journey toward understanding and embracing God's provision is both personal and communal. On a personal level, it requires a transformation of mindset—shifting from a mentality of scarcity to one of abundance. It involves recognizing that God is not limited in His resources or His desire to bless His children. As we align our lives with His principles—faith, stewardship, generosity, and ethical living—we position ourselves to receive His blessings in ways that exceed our expectations.

Diana Gadus, M.Ed.

On a communal level, the wealth and prosperity we receive are not for our benefit alone. They are meant to be shared, to uplift others, and to advance God's kingdom on earth. As we reflect on the stories and testimonies shared in this book, we see that true wealth is found in the impact we make, the lives we touch, and the legacy we leave behind. This perspective challenges us to use our resources wisely and purposefully, always with an eye toward how we can serve others and glorify God.

Reflecting on the content of this book, one can see that the path to prosperity is not a linear or straightforward one. It is a journey filled with opportunities for growth, challenges that refine our character, and moments that test our faith. Yet, through it all, the constant truth remains: God is faithful. His promises are sure, and His desire for us to live in abundance is unwavering.

This reflection is not just a summary of the principles we've discussed, but a call to action. It is a reminder that the truths we have uncovered are not meant to remain on the pages of this book but to be lived out daily. Whether you are just beginning your journey to financial freedom or are already experiencing the blessings of God's provision, the challenge is the same: to continue walking in faith, to steward what God has given you with wisdom and integrity, and to be a conduit of His blessings to others.

Diana Gadus, M.Ed.

As we close this book, I encourage you to carry these lessons with you, allowing them to shape your decisions, your relationships, and your view of God's generosity. Let them be a source of strength when you face difficulties, and a guide when you seek direction. Most importantly, let them deepen your relationship with the One who is the ultimate source of all blessings—our loving and faithful God.

In the end, wealth and prosperity are not just about financial gain but about living a life that reflects God's goodness and grace. It is about embracing the full life that Jesus spoke of in John 10:10: "I have come that they may have life, and have it to the full." May this fullness be your experience as you continue to trust in God's promises and walk in His ways.

With gratitude and hope,

Diana Gadus, M.Ed.

Diana Gadus, M.Ed.